It's Not Me, It's You!

Getting Over a Breakup in the Age of Technology

Matt Borer, Ph.D.

A Step by Step Guide to Getting Over a Break-up

It's Not Me, It's You!

*Getting over a breakup
in the age of technology.*

by
Matt Borer, Ph.D.

A Fat Zizzy Publication
Jacksonville, Florida

Edited by: Harmony Stalter/ Courtney Brasher
Typography: Justin Rigdon
Cover Photo: Carmen Marino
Author Photo: Carmen Marino
www.carmencayphotography.com

ISBN # 978-0-615-38923-3

Printed in the USA

I dedicate this book to my brilliant, beautiful wife Samantha, without whom there would be no book to publish, and no happy ending to celebrate.

Table of Contents

Acknowledgements

I would like to thank my wonderful wife Samantha for her unending support throughout my education and the writing of this book. I would like to thank my parents for their encouragement and love, and my brother Zack; the talented musician who has shown me it is always worth following your dreams, no matter how difficult the challenges may be.

Special thanks goes to Alison Kaplon, Kevin Lancaster, and my brother Zack for their unique contributions and help with the 8 year inception of this project.

Introduction

So my relationship is over… What do I do now? When will I feel better? Who can I turn to that understands how I feel? Is there anyone out there who can help me?

I know how you feel. I've been there, I am there, and I am always there to some extent. The pit of your stomach aches, your chest is tight and you just don't have the energy to do anything except wallow in your misery. "I want to talk, convince, beg, reconcile, and give up." I will so ANYTHING, to shake this feeling. Why don't they want to be with me? What went wrong? Why can't we talk? These questions have no clear right or wrong answer, but this book will ultimately help you to find a resolution to all of your relationship concerns.

You've tried to stay away from your ex, attempted to cry it out, but still nothing has worked. "But this feels like more than just a failed relationship!"

The need for this relationship is as strong as a drug; as appealing as a high. Unlike a drug, however, the fix is unobtainable and completely out of reach. Whether good or bad, the sting of a dissolved relationship is one of the most painful and difficult times in your life. It's time to recuperate, recover, and repair. It's time to focus on YOU again.

Because of today's technology, breaking up is a lot more complicated today than it was when your parents dated. This includes the constant access to the internet, the inescapable cell phone/PDA (iPhone and Blackberry, to name a few) each making it very difficult to stay away from the temptation of calling, e-mailing, texting, browsing a Facebook or MySpace page (a.k.a. "cyber-stalking) or instant messaging your ex. It used to be that people could just physically avoid one another to get over a breakup, but today, things are a lot more complicated. Disconnecting yourself from these technological complications is one of the most important steps to take in order to get over your ex. You may not know how to do this now, but you soon will. I am here to help you establish a roadmap to guide you through this process.

Nobody understands how you're feeling. Not your parents, teachers, or counselors. Not your brother or sister, and although your best friends say they understand, they just can't. Not unless they've been through it. I've been through it and so have the other people whose stories you will read in this book. We've been there. We've fought through the hurt, anger and pain. We've made it through to the other side of the heartache and were able to date again. Not every highlighted action discussed in this book will relate to you, but read, learn, and examine the steps that you think will be useful.

Following the roadmap will allow you to speed up the healing process and put you on the road to start feeling better immediately. The breakup stories weaved throughout the book will help illuminate the fact that you are not alone in this difficult period, and can help you sneak a glimpse of other's difficulties in their breakups. The breakup stories utilized in this book will allow me to provide you with a real life account of breakups in order to help you see the roadmap in action, to illustrate just how practical and effective this plan is. Together we are going to get you through this. You can be empowered!! You can be stronger!! You no longer have to be depressed!! Take the plan with you and follow these beginning steps.

I'm sure you have heard the saying "having the upper hand" in a relationship, and as of right now, this is not a position you find yourself in. Your relationship has ended and there is nothing you can do about it. You may be feeling depressed, anxious, nervous, as well as other emotional responses, all of which are painful and, depending on who's around, humiliating ways to react.

Together we can work to change these negative emotions into ones of empowerment and self-entitlement in order to help you grab the relational "upper hand" back. Read on and you will be given the secret tricks to re-position yourself to an angle that will place you in a win-win situation. Not only will you get over your ex, but you may have them begging to have you back.

Do I really need to have my ex's phone number stored in my cell? Do I need to have my ex as one of my friends on Myspace or Facebook? Do I need to continue to follow their Tweets from Twitter?

The answer is NO, and as you read on you will start to understand why the simple step of removing your ex's number from your cell phone, or taking them off of your friend list can be so important and empowering. The steps are simple. This book will show you how... Get ready to regain control over your emotions and overcome this emotional car wreck.

Read this book. Focus on you. Reflect on the case studies. But most importantly... **Don't Call! Don't Text! Don't IM!** You can do this! This book will help.

How to Approach your Breakup: Glamorization VS. Reality

Perception, exhaustion, glamorization, and technology are all forces that are going to attempt to lure you into the web of manipulation, guilt, and anxiety that your ex, whether knowingly or not, may compel you to become a part of. However, this so called web of desire only has the power to seduce you, if you leave yourself without the proper defenses for protection.

You need to be protected emotionally from the constant battle that may be waged between your heart and your brain, and, unfortunately, the two are unevenly matched. Although we would like to believe that rational thinking and common sense are traits that we possess, during times of emotional turmoil, our hearts and emotions take over and become the driving force behind our anxiety, fear, and impulsive behavior. This has potential to lead to great humiliation and hurt, and it is this book that can train your brain to take control over your current reality by putting your emotions and feelings on the backburner, even if only temporarily.

There are two concepts or actions that will play a very important part in your ability to overcome this breakup over the coming weeks and months.

The two concepts are *Intentional Behavior* and *Perception Puzzlement*. Amazingly, both of these variables are extremely important and constantly present in many things that you will inevitably think and potentially act upon over the next few weeks and months.

Intentional Behavior relates to any potential contact that you have, or will have with your ex, as well as the breakdown, or complication, of these encounters (i.e. phone calls, text message, e-mail, tweets, etc.). I'm sure that you have already experienced some of these things. Whether its been waiting for a phone call, checking an IM buddy list, viewing your ex's social website page, or any other contact, it is with almost a certainty that the interactive behavior that was once common place and routine (i.e. talking to your ex) is now a lot more complicated and anxiety riddled.

Have you run into your ex yet? Was this encounter at the mall, a bar, on campus, or some other place that the two of you would often hang out together? I can guess that this run in was NOT what you were hoping for, and probably left you feeling sad, angry, and confused.

The *Intentional Behavior* between you and your ex immediately changes once you break-up. The simple, everyday routine between the two of you, once the cornerstone of your relationship, is now an awkward, difficult situation. It doesn't seem to make sense how emotions can change in such a dramatic way overnight, and it hurts that the relationship has dissolved without you even realizing things were coming to an end. The missing link in this shocking turn of events is the fact that, in most cases, your ex has been changing his or her emotions for some time now, and while you are just now processing the shock of the breakup, your ex has had plenty of time to think and sort out his or her life without you.

You can't gain equal emotional footing with your ex, but you can change the *Intentional Behavioral* dynamic. It is not always important to understand why the breakup has happened, but instead it is important to focus on changing your behavior to get over this as fast as possible in order to regain control of your life.

Perception Puzzlement refers to the idea of how perception becomes clouded during a breakup. We often perceive our past relationship incorrectly, and often convince our-self of a positive perception of our ex in order to hold onto the possibility of reconciliation. While this is a nice thought, it is important to allow yourself, even if temporarily, to focus on the negative characteristics of your relationship and even your ex.

Go ahead. I am giving you permission. It is important to think about all the unpleasant details you so carefully hid somewhere in your mind. Human beings have an uncanny ability to fall into what I refer to as "trans without hypnosis" meaning that we are totally hypnotized by the positive moments with our ex, and totally oblivious to the negative parts. We get tunnel vision, and can't focus on the one thing that is most important right now; getting over this breakup.

Positive reflection of your relationship can be expressed later in the recovery process, but for now they will only confuse your emotions, making it more difficult to recover from this loss in your life. Retraining your mind to understand that in this situation, negative perception can lead to positive results, and that positive perception of your past relationship will only perpetuate your hurt and depression. This is crucial for your own mental health.

An example of this is if your ex has promised that they "need time apart, but will work to get back together." In these types of instances, it is almost always an unconscious tactic of your ex to use the "I need some space" excuse is just code for them breaking up with you. Because of this, it is crucial to shift your thoughts in the direction of thinking negatively about your ex and the "lines" that they have given you throughout this breakup.

You know the lines that I am referring to: the ones that you so desperately want to believe, but they just don't seem to be matching up with the actions of your ex. Looking at these situations with a positive perception (that your ex is actually going to do as they say) will only lead to potential disappointment, anxiety, and impatience. You need to work on your own time line in order to react to the confusion that your emotions are inflicting on your brain. We can do this by retraining your intellect and strength to focus a negative/realistic perception of your break up and ex, even if only momentarily.

With the concept of *Perception Puzzlement* comes the acceptance that the relationship that you were a part of did not work. Despite what many people say, good relationships do NOT end!! If they were "good" and "healthy," why would you be in this situation? It is time to begin your personal reclamation and look towards the future.

Coupled with your acceptance of the *Perception Puzzlement* must be a sense of realism that your ex hurt you, may have manipulated you, and that anyone who loved you would not hurt you the way that they have.

Taking Care of your Body

Often times, we focus so heavily on feeling better emotionally, that we forget that our bodies need to be treated with the same emphasis as the heart. I refer to the common forgetfulness and emotional eating as Fitness Failure. Basically these are the physical reactions in your body, often, which are the hardest of all of the issues to work through. This is partly because so much of it is tied into you being able to begin to get over your breakup. Therapists often say that a person is "somaticizing" their symptoms, which in English means that your feelings are causing your body to react in negative ways. There are benefits to a breakup, and although impossible to understand and realize now, it is important to keep hope and faith in yourself and your resolve.

To obtain these positive aspects of a breakup, it is crucial to take care of your health by employing several different eating habits that will ensure both mind and body health. This starts with understanding some of the basics of the human brain and how to maximize its effectiveness during this difficult time. When the brain produces a chemical called serotonin, tension is eased. When it produces dopamine or norepinephrine, we tend to think and act more quickly and are generally more alert. Eating carbohydrates alone seems to have a calming effect, while proteins increase alertness. While consuming complex carbohydrates, which raise the level of tryptophan (think about after thanksgiving dinner; relaxed?) in the brain, have a calming effect. Protein meals containing essential fatty acids and/or carbohydrates are recommended for increased alertness. Salmon and white fish are good choices that are rich in these essential fatty acids.

Avoid foods high in saturated fats; consumption of fried foods, such as chicken strips and French fries, leads to sluggishness, slow thinking, and fatigue. Fats inhibit the synthesis of neurotransmitters by the brain as they cause the blood cells to become sticky and to clump together, resulting in poor circulation. You especially need to consume more carbohydrates than protein if you are nervous and wish to become more relaxed, or eat more protein than carbohydrates if you are tired and wish to become more alert. A depressed person who needs his spirits lifted would benefit from eating foods like turkey and salmon, which are high in tryptophan and protein.

Beware: The body will react more quickly to the presence of sugar than it does to the presence of complex carbohydrates. The increase in energy supplied by the simple carbohydrates (present in foods with high sugar content) is quickly accompanied by fatigue and depression to the brain. A handful of a Multi cereal adds folic acid, which can help fend off the blues. Those with low levels of the nutrient experience more symptoms of depression, a study in the Journal of Epidemiology and Community Health suggests, and a folic acid deficiency may prevent your antidepressants from working.

A final, and simple eating habit that can help you regain your sunny disposition is adding a few egg yolks to your diet. Egg yolks contain choline, a mood enhancer. Being low on this nutrient may lead to feeling anxious, and as you and I both know, anxiety is the last thing that you need more of at the moment.

In addition to your diet, your thoughts, emotions, and behavior all affect body chemistry. For instance, relaxation produces the chemical norepinephrine, with which low levels are implicated in depression. Also, exercise has been shown to produce another chemical known as endorphins, which will help with depression, anxiety, sleep, and sexual activity. So, besides eating certain foods, relaxation and exercise are things that we do that can also affect the level and activity of these chemicals.

Thomas Jefferson wrote that most people feel about as happy as they make up their minds to be. After a breakup, there is a period of time where we want to wallow in our own misery, and just feel sad. (*Think about the depressing music that you've been voluntarily listening to within the confines of your private space*). While a small amount of self -pity never hurt anyone, there is a limit, and this limit needs to be defined.

If you are reading this book, the time for the self pity and introversion is now over. It is now time to take a deep breath, (seriously, take a deep breath), sit up (I'm not kidding), go stand in front of a mirror, (yes, I know you look like crap right now), and say these words out loud to yourself; "It is time to stop wallowing, and start recovering."

I want you to say this out loud three times. While this may seem ridiculous, there is real science behind this type of activity, and this form of self- talk has been proven to effectively help all kinds of people, with all kinds of issues, move on from their discomfort and sadness, and begin to reclaim his or her life. This form of therapy is called *cognitive therapy* and it is basically a relatively short-term form of psychotherapy based on the concept that the way we think about things affects how we feel emotionally.

Cognitive therapy focuses on present thinking, behavior, and communication rather than on past experiences and is oriented toward problem solving. Cognitive therapy has been applied to a broad range of problems including depression, anxiety, fears, eating disorders, substance abuse, and personality problems. The exercise I just described, if done properly, is going to begin to transform you from a feeling of helplessness, to a feeling of empowerment and strength.

Most people have never heard of serotonin management, or even considered it at all, except for medications.

Serotonin management involves paying attention to the little things that make you feel good and systematically including them in your daily routine. We know, instinctively, that pampering ourselves is a pathway to a sense of well being, but we may not take time to schedule pleasant surroundings, favorite music or food, or even quality time with loved ones into our daily agenda. Just getting out of bed and into a warm shower elevates serotonin levels, making it easier to get into a positive, constructive frame of mind. And generally speaking, depression (if it is mild enough) can sometimes be managed without prescribed medications.

Aerobic exercise, watching your carbohydrate and alcohol consumption, getting up early and moving, even if you don't feel like it, forcing structure on your life, using meditation and imagery (if you can concentrate, which depends on how depressed you are), and seeking a support group or psychotherapy, have all proved helpful.

No matter what the reason is for feeling the way that you currently do, whether it is a chemical imbalance or just situational depression, the steps can be very beneficial in the mind and body healing process.

All of us go through feelings of sadness, disappointment, anxiety or despair. Feeling depressed or sad during a particularly difficult situation can be natural and even healthy. It may help you to overcome emotional challenges while allowing you to increase some creative problem-solving techniques.

The down time resulting from these feelings may provide an opportunity for healing insight, reevaluation and transformation. A few blue days grant us an excuse to slow down and re-program. Following these simple life changes along with the steps laid out in this book, will help place you in a more spiritual, reflective, and empowered state to get over this breakup.

Do Not Glamorize, Do Not Glamorize, Do Not Glamorize!!!

Eat	Don't Eat
Carbohydrates (grains, rice, pasta)	**Fried foods**
Protein (salmon, white fish, turkey)	**Foods high in saturated fat** (bacon, sausage, butter)
Foods high in folic acid (leafy green vegetables)	**Alcohol** (while it may feel better for a minute, you will hurt worse in the morning)
Complex Carbohydrates (Brown rice, potatoes, whole grain cereal)	**Sugary Foods** (candy bars, gummi bears, soda pop)
Chocolate (it's important to not deprive yourself of chocolate in moderation)	**Caffeine** (for the addicts, limit it to one cup of coffee)
Vegetables (do you really need examples?)	**Refined Carbohydrates** (white rice, white pasta, high fructose corn syrup)
Egg yokes (within limit)	

Confidence is Crucial

Self-confidence, coupled with your ability to be an active participant in a relationship, is among the first things to disappear after a break up. It is such an ego blow to be "dumped," and a lack of confidence can really hinder your ability to recuperate from the breakup. With a loss of self-esteem, often, comes a lack of insight into your ex's previous signs of rejection toward your relationship (and you in general). A missed late night phone call, not coming home one night, or a strange text message on his or her phone, are often signs that your ex may have lost interest in the relationship, but while lacking a significant sense of control and confidence, often times these

unfortunate gestures and suspicions go
overlooked.

The quality of people's relationships tends to
fluctuate over time. Unfortunately, most
disagreements and conflicts of interest are evident
even in the closest of relationships.

Almost universally, couples promise to love
one another "for better or worse" and friends
promise to stick together "through thick and thin."
Nonetheless, it is clear that people find it easier to
adore their significant other when things are going
well in the relationship.

Because rejection from significant others can
undermine self-esteem, people interpret actions
that occur in the relationship for evidence of
whether a romantic partner loves them or whether
a friend accepts them (Dehart, Pelham, & Murray,
2000).

Obviously, when a break up occurs, it is very
difficult to interpret any situation clearly,
specifically what went wrong in your relationship,
and the rejection can powerfully undermine your
self-esteem.

The beginning stages are crucial in retraining your brain and self worth in order to recover and learn from both the mistakes and triumphs of your past relationships.

When you are a part of a couple, you begin to think differently than you once did while single. You ask your partner questions like "What should we do tonight," or "Do you want to go to class together," and even questions like "Would you mind if I had a girls/guys night out tonight?" The longer that you are in the relationship, the stronger the cognitive pull of your partners wishes and desires become your own. Your brain actually begins to think differently than ever before, and in healthy couples this can be an asset, but in unhappy couples, this retraining of the brain can be really hard to get over, even potentially damaging.

So the question becomes, "How do I change my pattern of thinking and regain my independent thoughts and feelings?" This is a great question because it is the heart of the self-confidence and empowerment ideals that you need to instill within yourself in order to get over your ex.

An important aspect of confidence retooling is the ability to *appear* unscathed and ok.

Your friends are going to continuously ask you, "How are you?" "Are you ok?" "How are you holding up?" "Is there anything I can do for you?" But as we all know, and your friends know, you are hurting. Your heart and your confidence are wounded, but allowing yourself to play the role of a victim will only bring on sympathetic gestures from those around you.

Pity is not what you need. You need support from your friends and family to help you to get back out there and continue living your life in a positive, healthy way.

The way to do this is to play the role of an optimistic, self-reflective person who is not afraid to explain his or her situation, but will not be goaded into playing the victim for all to see. If you appear confident, others will relate to you in that manner. Do not be afraid to explain to your friends and family that you are attempting to regain your confidence and self-esteem, and you would appreciate any help that they could provide you with in obtaining that goal.

There comes a point when empathy from others becomes a burden and roadblock to your recovery; that time is now, and because of this, it is important to appear confident, composed, and rejuvenated.

Time is one of the key elements of complete recovery over emotional hurt, fortunately, outward optimism is a lot easier to accomplish AND can be attained immediately. I understand that you may not be able to do this instantly, but since you are now reading this book, I have a feeling that you need something to kick-start some kind of change into your life.

The longer you can act confident and self-assured, the more that the attributes of these qualities will begin to stick, and become a part of who you are. Acting confident will create confidence. It is crucial, however, to understand that you must continue to follow the steps in this book and allow for your feelings to be expressed.

I am in no way asking you to repress the feelings of hurt and betrayal – they are very important to work through. I am, however, asking you to begin to move in a direction of self healing and personal confidence boosting.

Confidence is the key! What will bother your ex more than the sight of a confident, active, healthy person that is no longer consumed with the damage that afflicted them during their break up? Things will get better and you have the power and control to make it happen.

Why is it so Hard to Get Over & What Will Help

This is obviously one of the worst feelings you have EVER had. It can seem worse than the feeling associated with a bad grade, losing a competition, and even a death for some people. It's a feeling that you just cannot seem to escape. It will not leave you alone. It follows you from the moment you wake up in the morning until you go to sleep at night. It is a cloud that shadows your every waking move, paining your head, chest and heart. But why is it so bad? It's just a break up! This isn't the end of my life!

Although all of these are rational, true thoughts, unfortunately, your heart and emotions don't always follow the intellectual clarity of your brain. It is this disconnect that makes the feeling of a break up so difficult.

In the therapeutic fields, there is a guidebook to psychological disorders called the *DSM-IV TR*. Professionals use this book to help diagnose their clients and as a reference to issues that may be contributing to a person's behavior. One of these disorders is called Obsessive Compulsive Disorder. I use this example because one of the major symptoms of the disorder is a compulsion to act on irrational obsessions without any basis in reality.

Obsessive-compulsive disorder (OCD), a type of anxiety disorder, is a potentially disabling illness that traps people in endless cycles of repetitive thoughts and behaviors. People with OCD are plagued by recurring and distressing thoughts, fears or images (obsessions) that they cannot control.

The anxiety (nervousness) produced by these thoughts leads to an urgent need to perform certain rituals or routines (compulsions). The compulsive rituals are performed in an attempt to prevent the obsessive thoughts or make them go away.

Although the ritual may make the anxiety go away temporarily, the person must perform the ritual again when the obsessive thoughts return. This OCD cycle can progress to the point of taking up hours of the person's day and significantly interfering with normal activities. People with OCD may be aware that their obsessions and compulsions are senseless or unrealistic, but they cannot stop themselves. Why do I bring this up?

It is this senselessness of thoughts that parallel much of the thinking that you engage in after a break up. Whether it is the glamorization of your relationship, the thoughts of regret and self blame, or even the anxious ideas that somehow seeing or speaking to your ex will lead to a getting back together, these all are similar to the obsessions and compulsions that a person with OCD suffers from.

Luckily, these behaviors differ in a dramatic way from a person suffering from OCD. You are most likely not suffering from a lack of serotonin in your brain, as someone with OCD patients are, but you are suffering from a broken heart.

Unfortunately, these two ailments often have similar symptoms. So how do you rectify these feelings, whether they are feelings of obsessions and compulsions or those of depression?

The Stages of Grief and How They Relate to a Breakup

During a breakup, the loss of the relationship is often the hardest thing to get over. For so long you have been committed to a person and the ideas and patterns that accompany that relationship. But now, you no longer have that piece in your life, and it can lead to a very negative feeling, similar to the loss of a loved one.

Dr. Elisabeth Kubler-Ross has named five stages of grief that people go through following a serious loss. Understanding these stages can help you to understand that what you are feeling is normal and natural, as well as identifying where you currently are in the process, and where you ultimately hope to be. The five stages of grief with a breakup spin are:

1) **Denial and Isolation**- At first we tend to deny the loss has taken place, and may withdraw from our usual social contacts. This stage may last a few days, weeks, or months (*although if you follow the steps in this book, this should be much faster to get over*)

2) **Anger** The grieving person may be furious at the person who inflicted the hurt, or at the world for letting it happen. He or she may be angry at themselves for letting the breakup happen, even if realistically, nothing could have stopped it.

3) **Bargaining**- The grieving person may make attempt to make deal with their ex in order to rekindle the relationship, often times, presenting sex with the hopes that the physicality between the two will help the couple reconnect.

4) **Depression**- The person may feel numb, although, anger and sadness may remain underneath, often times, causing a lack of control over emotions, and in the case of a breakup, often times contributing to the possibility of making irrational, and bad decisions.

5) <u>**Acceptance**</u>- This is when the anger, sadness and hurt have diminished, and you are able to look back at the relationship and realize that the breakup was the best thing that could have happened, and that there are many positive ideas and memories that can be taken from your past relationship and applied to the rest of your life.

The stages of grief fit nicely into the Breakup Plan, because they give a person permission to feel upset, angry, depressed etc., while also laying out a direct plan or steps with which to use to ultimately get to the point of acceptance. Understanding what you are going through will help you adjust to each set of emotions that surface, as well as help to provide you with a roadmap to follow to the ultimate path of healing and happiness.

Don't underestimate the power of a breakup, and don't allow anyone else to diminish the feelings that you are having. The steps outlined in this book will get you to final stage of grief, acceptance, and allow you the happiness and empowerment that you deserve.

Clinical Depression vs. Just Feeling Down

Sadness, anger and depression are all completely normal feelings to experience during a breakup. There is, however, a difference between feeling sad and being clinically depressed. There are certain symptoms that may help you identify if your feelings are symptoms of the breakup or whether they are symptoms of something that requires an appointment with a physician.

As with any ailment, depression is to be treated the same way that you would treat strep throat or an ear infection: a simple checkup with your family doctor to evaluate your symptoms and rule out any other issues that may be causing some of your depressive symptoms. But first, some self-evaluation is necessary to see where you might be on the depressive scale.

When depressed, there are things that therapeutic professionals call "vegetative signs" that can help you and your doctor tell how depressed you may be. There are several important questions to ask yourself as well as your parent or guardian, or close friend when, and if, you are feeling depressed.

1) Have there been any changes in my sleeping patterns since the breakup? (Example: Are you waking up several times at night thinking about your ex or having a hard time falling asleep because your brain won't shut off?)

2) Has your appetite been affected or changed since your breakup? (Example: Have you lost your appetite, or are you uncharacteristically overeating?)

3) Have there been any changes in your sexual desire since your breakup (Example: You seem to have lost interest in having sex?)

4) Have you had any difficulty tasting your food since your breakup? (Example: Sometimes when we are depressed all our food tastes bland and lacks flavor)

5) Have you noticed any significant memory loss? (Example: Are you having a hard time concentrating and are you forgetful when it comes to daily activities?)

It is vitally important to answer these questions honestly and to discuss them with your parent/ guardian, or close friend, especially if you have answered "yes" to any of the questions. As was discussed earlier, in your process of recovery, taking care of your health, both physical and emotional, is extremely important.

In the case that you may be more than situationally sad, your recovery process will not be able to be fully achieved without support from other professionals, such as a doctor and possibly a counselor. If this chapter is speaking to you, you have nothing to be ashamed of, and more importantly, you have the advantage of being able to identify the underlying cause of your sadness. Do not be embarrassed.

Be brave, and seek the help that you may need. This book can only help you fully, if you're as healthy as you can be. See a doctor AND read this book! Together the combination of these two things can be immensely successful in getting you over your breakup.

The Plan

&

Case Studies

Case Studies

The case studies included between chapters are real examples of people just like you, who during their breakups did everything possible to make getting over their ex and moving on as difficult as possible. Some of these examples will speak directly to your experience and some may not, however, it is important to read each case and identify each person's difficulties in getting over their relationship and to learn from the skills and steps that I have put forth to help each one of these people.

I will show you how these people should have interacted with their ex in order to maximize their long term happiness, and I will highlight the ways that the breakup steps that I have outlined, ultimately, put these people on the right track to recovery. Ultimately, these steps will do the same for you. Remember, none of these steps are easy, and in fact there will be times when you feel that the steps are unfair and even impossible, but keep reading and you will start to see that you can do this; you can get over your ex, just as the people in these case studies did.

1

The Cell Phone Curse

How many contacts do you have saved in your phone? 50? 100? 200? There's no way you would you know the majority of people's phone numbers without it. Chances are your cell phone has been the main form of communication that you and your ex have had outside of your face-to-face time throughout your relationship.

You have his or her home number saved, his or her work number saved, all of his or her cells saved, each taking up crucial room in your cell that could now be reserved for new contacts to be saved in. The cell phone, although, in my opinion, the greatest convenience of modern time is also the biggest curse during a relationship breakup.

You have the chance and opportunity of potential contact with your ex, all day, and everyday, no matter where you are. The mall, class, work, and even the worst place to have an opportunity to contact or be contacted: **THE BAR!!!!**

"I want to see them, text them my feelings, tell them to screw off, and I can. I have the phone...I'll just call, or even better, I'll text." (*You can then play the awful waiting game to see when and if your ex will text back*). When you are getting over a breakup, you often make some stupid decisions and assumptions about yourself and your ex.

This is especially true when it comes to the idea that your ex wants to not only talk to you, but wants to get into a conversation about your relationship: what went wrong, how can it be fixed, etc. This seemingly good idea to contact your ex can pop into your head when you least expect it. Unfortunately, it is almost never the case that conversing with your ex will turn out well, and usually the last thing your ex wants to do is talk.

In my own experience with my clients and myself, even if you are able to have a conversation with your ex, the conversation almost always brings more hurt, depression and a diminished feeling of self-worth. But we do it over and over and over again, until the person we loved and still love, become frustrated and mean.

You've gone back and forth, the anxiety pushing you to call or text, and your ex is emotionally and psychologically abusing you with their constant rejections and mean, insensitive words. "Forget this, I don't need this abuse." But we keep going back anyway. The cell phone is the simplest way to either continue or interrupt this awful pattern. **"STEP AWAY FROM THE CELL PHONE!!!"**

Are you ready to take the first and most important aspect to the recovery and ultimately the reclamation and rediscovery of you? Buckle up, here we go.
- Step 1) Pick up your cell phone.
- Step 2) Open up your contacts
- Step 3) Find your ex's numbers
- Step 4) **Delete, Delete, Delete!**

It is important to delete all of your ex's numbers in your phone, even if you know their number by heart. Not having the number in your phone creates an extra step to making the call, and any barrier between you and talking to your ex is a good thing. It slows the process down and gives you a chance for second thoughts before you call or text.

You may be asking, "How would not talking to him or her help me to feel better and not worse?" While logically, everything you have been taught is that communication about your relationship and working out your difficulties with your partner is the best way to solve your issues. However, in the case of a breakup, all logic gets thrown out the window.

The importance of breaking off communication with your ex is rooted in the theory that as long as you are preoccupied with any form of actively engaging in a relationship with your ex, the harder it is and longer it will take for you to begin to move to a place where you can reclaim yourself as an individual. As long as you are communicating with your ex, you cannot clear your mind of the hurt and uncertainty from your breakup. As long as you are fully pre-occupied with your lost relationship, you will never be able to focus on getting better.

It's time to take the steps to no longer allow yourself to be known as your ex's boyfriend or girlfriend. It's time that people once again know you by your true identity: the individual that you know you are (and that your friends and family remember, and know you can be). While all of this sounds good, this is easier said than done. Here is how to do it...

Your smart phone provides you with instant access to virtually anything you can imagine, instantly, and while these gadgets can be one of the coolest, most convenient possessions you may own, they can also lead to making the recovery from your breakup a lot harder to deal with. So many times, relationships are allowed to linger, hang around, and loiter in your life. Break up.... Get back together... Break up....Get back together.... And on and on it goes, each time opening up a new, fresh, and deeper emotional wound than the time before.

Couples often end up falling into a pattern of not only accepting their misery, but also beginning to rely on the comfort of that same misery. This pattern has become so much of whom you have become, that even the thought of losing the unhappiness is scary. But fear itself cannot comfort you, or keep you in a pattern of receiving way less than you deserve. Only your pride and self-assurance can move you to the level of comfort, allow you to heal, and ultimately move on. The cell phone is a tremendous impediment to getting over your breakup, especially with the convenience and ease of texting.

The added complication to calling these days is now known to us all as the text message. The beauty and tragedy of texting is the ability to quickly contact someone at virtually any point…silently.

It is great for the library, the club, work, as well as countless other situations, however, while the ability to text words is convenient, words can be misleading and have unintended consequences, especially when you aren't able to perceive the emotion behind those words. This is almost always the case when it comes to texting.

Think about the text you got that's sounded way worse than it actually was meant to be, or the text that was accidentally written in all caps, and you thought you were being yelled at.

When you are already an emotional wreck, any communication misunderstanding can have dire emotional penalties, especially when you can't immediately clear up the potential miscommunications, as is often the problem with texting. Deleting your ex's number from your cell phone ads a small, yet significant, barrier to the ease and simplicity of sending a text.

I'm sure by now you have found yourself sending a text to your ex, and then waiting, anxiously, for any response. The problem with this is that you find yourself in a lose/lose situation. If your ex does not text you back you feel terrible, angry, worried and anxious. If your ex does text you back, but the message isn't what you had expected or hoped for, you feel depressed, sad, and nervous.

Either way, the emotional and often physical reaction is negative. You may ask, "But what if the response is positive and my ex does want to talk?" The fact of the matter is that while this is a possibility, all of the other possible alternatives are more likely, and therefore it is in your best interest to avoid the situation all together. Put yourself in a win/win scenario. If you don't text your ex, you avoid the potential pain and anxiety of not receiving the text you hope for, and, it is more likely than not that your ex will text you, nervous about your recent lack of interest.

Now this leaves the issue of if and when your ex calls or texts you, and how, if you have deleted their number from your phone, will you know it is them calling or texting? The answer to this is that you won't, and here we have uncovered the key to the equation. If you haven't screened your calls before, it is time to start screening them now. For at least one month, possibly more depending on the situation, you are going to have to screen your calls, and if you don't recognize the number, let it go to voicemail.

What happens if and when my ex texts me? Unfortunately, the only thing that you can control is your own actions, and there is a good chance that you will eventually hear from your ex, either by a call or a text. You have two choices in this situation, with both options being difficult. You can either erase the message, both voicemail and text before you have a chance to hear or read the message, or, you can read the message (at your own risk) and resist the temptation to text back or return the call. Now, while there are two choices here, the lesser of the two evils is to **delete, delete, delete**, before you have the opportunity to make a decision that you may later regret.

Look at it this way... You can listen to the voice mail or read the text message and potentially restart the whole pattern of hurt, disappointment, and anxiety, with the small chance that you will hear or see what you have been hoping to read or hear for weeks: that your ex wants you back. Or, you can delete the message before reading or listening and guarantee yourself a continued pathway to independence and recovery.

The point that you must remember when making any decision about your actions, or inactions in a breakup, is a point that I will make throughout this book: Healthy and happy couples do not intentionally hurt each other, and if the relationship was meant to be, then the relationship would not have ended.

You deserve better than someone who will hurt you, and you are bigger as an individual than you ever were as a couple. So, with that said...drop the cell phone, and cut off the tie that is holding you back, these ties that are binding you to a relationship that you no longer have any control over. Take control by allowing you to not make that call or send that text. You have to start somewhere. Why not here?

My Story

I felt that it was important for me to share my own story, not only to gain the credibility of everyone reading this book, but for you, the reader to understand that there is a method to my madness. My breakup and everything that I did wrong during my six-month recovery process was the inspiration for the steps that I have outlined successfully for many others, and ultimately will help you to regain control and recover from your breakup.

My breakup was facilitated by a poor decision that, ultimately, cost me my relationship. My girlfriend of a year and a half as well as myself, were preparing to each go our separate ways for spring break. Sara was going to Jamaica, and I was going to Cancun for the week with several of my friends. Sara was going with a group of her girlfriends. The night before she left for her trip she asked me a question: "All of my friends are single, and what happens if they are all hooking up with guys and I want to kiss someone?"

Although a bit surprised, I always believed that we had a strong, trusting relationship, and a kiss would make very little difference in the grand scheme of our relationship. (Often times, in relationships we make decisions without fully thinking them through). I did, however, stipulate that if she were to stray, that she shouldn't do it with anyone from our school and to not discuss it with me when she returned (Ignorance is bliss).

The day after we both got back, Sara came over to my parent's house, and told me that she needed to speak to me. She explained that she had strayed, and with someone from our school. (The reason I am supplying such a detailed background, is because these events ultimately led to the breakup and consequently all of the mistakes that I made). Through tears, we discussed what happened with Sara, and decided to stay together. We returned to school as solid as we were prior to spring break (Or so I thought).

After returning to school, there were several unexplainable coincidences that should have tipped me off to the fact that there was trouble in paradise, the first of which was as anxiety inducing as anything I had experienced in my life up to that point. Sara had gone out drinking with some friends and had made plans to come spend the night at my place afterwards. Around 11 pm, I got a call from Sara telling me that she would be over in the next half hour or so. As the clock hit 11:30, and then 12:00, and then at 12:15, I started to worry.

The obvious thing to do was to call her cell phone, which I did numerous times, and each time the phone went straight to voicemail. When 1:00 am rolled around and I still hadn't heard from Sara, I instant messaged her roommate who told me that she hadn't heard from Sara either. By 2:00

I was out of my mind worried, and decided to go out driving and make sure that there weren't any accidents that Sara may have been involved in. While driving around like a maniac, my phone finally rang and it was Sara on the other end. I yelled, "Where the hell were you?" but didn't hear her answer. I was so relieved that she was ok, that at that moment, I wasn't interested in the answer.

Sara met me at my apartment and explained that she had been distracted at her sorority house and lost track of time. Sara then started crying, which she blamed on feeling terrible that I was so worried about her, but I thought the tears were a bit fishy. I wasn't sure why she was crying if she truthfully had just been held up at home, but I chose to ignore this fact, along with so many other signs that Sara was giving, telling me that the relationship was on thin ice.

Several days went by, and things seemed to be going pretty well; our routine was back on track, and we both seemed happy to have put Spring break behind us and to be moving forward with the relationship. One night I asked Sara if "She was feeling better about the two of us?"

Let's just say that I didn't get the answer that I was hoping for... Sara decided that it was time for a break with the promise that she would put 100 percent of her effort to working through her issues and getting back together. I was devastated, and from this point, my mistakes and pathetic attempts at reclaiming my relationship began.

My biggest problem from the start of my breakup was the false hope that Sara and I were actually going to get back together. With this in mind, I was constantly waiting for her to call, checking my e-mail for a message from her, and asking all of my friends with whom she was in contact with for any information that could help me get Sarah back.

Within the first day of our breakup, I had broken three of the cardinal rules when recovering from a breakup. If I had initially made the choice to totally disassociate myself from my ex, I wouldn't have been waiting by the phone because even if it rang I wouldn't have picked it up. Secondly, if Sara had sent an e-mail, it would have immediately been deleted, and by quickly choosing my DL, I would have avoided the humiliation of allowing all of our mutual friends the opportunity to be a witness to my emotional catastrophe.

I continued to follow the same path that I had traveled during my relationship, all while hoping, wishing, and even praying to run into my ex so that we could finally have the opportunity to have the conversation that would convince her that we should still be together. If she would just listen, she would understand that we should be together, and she would see how badly I needed her and how much I loved her. As I had planned, I ran into Sara whenever I felt the need, and each time she gave me the same look of apathy and pity. I was like a pathetic puppy dog, panting after my owner with a tennis ball. I would have happily fetched any bone that Sara could have thrown me.

My main issue, that was facilitating the breaking of rule after rule, was the false sense of reality that my vulnerable mind was living in. I truly believed that Sara and I were going to get back together, and the more that I made myself visible, the more she would want to be with me.

Because we had a set routine of meeting at certain places on campus between classes, I knew where she would be. Therefore, I knew that if I needed to see her, I knew where to find her. With the irrational thoughts that were consuming me at this point of my breakup, I wanted to see her as often as possible, but each time that I "ran" into her I ended up feeling way more depressed and pathetic.

At the time, I was bartending at a popular pub in town that was frequented by Sara's group of friends. One night Sara showed up with the person that she had been dating, who consequently was the same person with whom she made out with on spring break. As upset as this made me, it was my first point of realization that my relationship may be past the point of reclamation or reconciliation. The next day I "ran" into Sara and asked her never to come to the bar again, because it was too difficult for me to work with her there.

This was the first positive step that I took towards my recovery from my breakup. By telling her that she could no longer come to the bar where I worked, I drew a significant line in the sand that separated where I had been and where I needed to go on a journey to renewal. This journey led to a renewal of my spirit and a revitalization of my pride.

Unfortunately, I took several more pathetic attempts at reconciliation. During this lowest season of my life, I actually got down on my hands and knees and begged for Sara back. It wasn't until after that low moment that I finally got to a point that I could start to take stock of what choices I needed to make to ultimately recover. Unfortunately for me, this was also her decision when she told me that we could no longer talk and she essentially wanted nothing to do with me.

My pitiful and humiliating endeavor to reconcile had, once again, provided my ex with another opportunity to reject me. She not only kicked me to the curb, but I waited for the door to hit me on the ass before actually leaving.

From that point on, I started to formulate the steps that have contributed to the effectiveness and importance of this book. I started to walk a different path to class, went to different bars, took down all of the pictures of Sara and I, hung out with only friends that were mine before the relationship, and stopped checking my e-mail with the hopes of receiving a message from my ex. For all intents and purposes, I became virtually invisible to my ex.

These steps and my ultimate course of action finally freed me to start living for myself again. I still missed my ex, but the steps that I outlined for myself and were actively engaged in were my main concern. I had the freedom of knowing that I wouldn't run into Sara, and I had the knowledge that she would no longer have the privilege of seeing me.

I was a ghost. I spent countless hours revamping and preparing myself to get back on the dating scene. "Stop feeling depressed and start having fun" was the mantra that I repeated over and over again. I, finally, felt empowered about my life and I reclaimed the control that I had lost.

Although my pride and ego had taken a beating, they weren't dead. I, finally, reclaimed the strength to bounce back.

My story, although painful at times to recount, is just one example of a tough breakup situation. The steps, however, propelled me to a position of empowerment and direction with which to start to meet new people and experience new situations. I DID IT, SO CAN YOU!!!!

2

Internet Angst

Our lives revolve around being online. With DSL, cable modems and other high speed connections, Smartphone, iPhones, Wi-Fi, etc., we are constantly connected and available for potentially destructive encounters with our ex. Home, school, work, the library, we are always connected and always ready for a good dose of cyber stalking. You know you've done it. We all have. Often times, after a breakup we go crazy. We do things that no logical person would do and the internet makes it so gosh darn easy. We can all be cyber-stalkers, and we've all been there at some point. It seems that our former flames never seem to change their numerous passwords, which they of course gave to us when we were together.

So many people now have websites to constantly browse, our buddy list is always up, Skype contacts are constantly ringing, Google and yahoo messenger are always connected, and our Facebook contacts are always available in real time. All of these potential connections causing similar obsessive thoughts; hoping and praying that our ex will show up online and instant message us. The shear simplicity and availability of this resource is scary, and can make getting over a relationship much more difficult then in the past.

Technology has so many great uses, including the connection to many potential daters. But this importance is far outweighed by the destructive nature that it can have on your psyche when getting over a breakup. As our mothers used to say, "If you can't play nice, don't play at all."

During a breakup it is crucial to avoid destructive behavior and temptation, including things such as im-ing and e-mailing your ex. And if you can't stop these actions then you have to take the computer out of the equation until you can learn to "play nice."

The first and major step is taking your ex off of your buddy list and erasing them from your e-mail address book. MySpace pages and Facebook accounts present a uniquely tricky predicament, in that deleting your ex from your friends, not only hinders your ex from seeing your status updates, but also deprives you of finding out what it is he or she is up to.

Deciding the proper time to delete your ex from your friend list is a difficult one, but it is also crucial, and the reason is this, manipulation is the name of the game during a breakup, and there is no easier way for your ex to manipulate a situation, than by fabricating all kinds of bragging, narcissistic claims about themselves, with the goal of hurting you and self serving them. I'm sure you have already experienced your ex posting pictures or comments of, or about all of the fun he or she is having without you, all with the purpose of hurting you and pouring salt into an already freshly opened wound.

The solution to this problem is to delete your ex from your friends, and if need be, erase any friend that may provide you with easy access to their page. That means that if your best friends MySpace account has your ex as one of her or his friends, delete them, even if only temporarily.

For the same reason that erasing an ex's name from your cell phone is important, the same holds true for the internet. Not only will not having the power to control what you see frustrate your ex, it will also provide you with control to not allow them to view your page as well. You will now have control over what you see, or don't see, and a sense of empowerment that you will need to embrace and accept to be successful in this program.

Because of the importance and everyday necessity of the computer, it may be impossible to entirely eliminate it from use. It is, however, important to prioritize your goals when going on-line, and to make sure that there is a purpose to your browsing. Set time limits for your projects, work, and entertainment, and stick to them. Don't allow yourself to find that you have time to kill, so "Maybe I'll try to contact my ex or maybe just see if they're online." Cut off the possibility of connection.

What about if my ex tries to contact me? Well this takes us into the ever important and virtually impossible topic of controlling our ex's initial manipulation over our emotions and feelings. It never fails that the second you are having a good moment, day, or even week, your ex will send you that ever elusive e-mail or instant message that you so strongly craved. This may be the hardest thing you will have to do in your reconnection with yourself but; **Don't Read It. Erase It. Erase It. Erase It.**

I'm sure you are asking yourself, "but what if it's important and my ex needs me?" The answer to this is that your ex lost the privilege of having your shoulder to lean on and if there was really a problem, your ex has multiple ways to contact you that are more direct than an e-mail or instant message.

If you have a buddy list, block yourself from being seen by your ex's computer. Nothing good will come out of your ex's pathetic attempts to "Try to be Friends," or "See how you're doing," or "Wanting to tell you the good news," Or "I need to tell you the bad news." (This, by the way, is the ultimate in the breakup manipulation.) Don't fool yourself. This empty attempt to reconnect is nothing but an attempt to work through your ex's guilt. Nothing will make your ex feel worse than a total loss of contact with the person they once loved, and let's be honest with yourself: it is time you started thinking about you, and nobody else.

Your feelings need to be attended to and it's time you paid attention to the person reading this book. Remember, there is nothing worse than contributing to the destruction of your own psyche. Your ex has done enough; don't join in on the party. You're invited to a party of a whole different caliber. A party celebrating your independence, an opportunity for bigger and better things than your ex could ever have offered.

This may be hard to see now, but think about the party or dance that your friend dragged you to that you ended up having a great time at. I'm your friend dragging you to the party celebrating you and your new single life.

Computer Disconnection

Rachel and her boyfriend had been dating for a year and a half, and although things were rocky at times, they always appeared to have a solid relationship. Both Rachel and her boyfriend were popular in school, active in clubs and had great social lives. Sexually the two were very compatible and they both had very similar hopes for the future.

With the love and support of his girlfriend, Rachel's boyfriend decided to transfer to a University within the same city to further his education. Unfortunately for Rachel, this meant that she and her boyfriend were going to be spending less time together during the week, but would still be able to hang out with each other and their friends on the weekend.

Things appeared to be fine; the couple seemed to be doing well until Rachel's boyfriend started to exhibit symptoms of being really stressed with school. He had been spending a lot of time with his study group, including going out during the week, and spending a lot of time over at the study group's respective houses.

As time went on, Rachel, although hurting, continued to support her boyfriend and his continued educational goals. One day, as Rachel was chatting online with some of her friends, she got an e-mail from her boyfriend. Not concerned about the content, Rachel opened the e-mail thinking that her boyfriend had made plans for the two of them for the weekend.

To Rachel's dismay, her boyfriend explained to Rachel that the two of them had grown apart over the last couple of months and felt as though the couple needed some space to "figure things out." In obvious shock, Rachel immediately called her boyfriend's cell phone to attempt to understand where her boyfriend could possibly be coming from.

When Rachel's boyfriend picked up the phone, he was in a loud environment with a lot of female voices in the background. Rachel, with tears in her eyes and hurt in her voice, begged her boyfriend to reconsider, "Please come over after work so we can talk about this!!" With a mild sense of contempt in his voice, he told Rachel "I have other plans tonight but will call you tomorrow and we can talk."

Although upset that she would have to wait a day, (which we all know was probably going to be the longest, loneliest, most vulnerable day of Rachel's life) she felt a sense of relief to, if nothing else, have the opportunity to find out what went wrong and attempt to reconnect with her now ex-boyfriend. "All I need to do is talk to him and he'll remember what we had together."

A very important aspect of a breakup takes place in the initial phase of the conflict. When someone breaks up with you, it's crucial to take a day or two to contemplate and process this life changing event. Right after the shock of getting dumped, you can't think straight, You are an emotional basket case, and nothing can be accomplished positively in that frame of mind.

For Rachel, it was important that she call her ex after receiving the break up e-mail, but after her advances to see her ex were rejected, Rachel should have cognitively stepped away from the situation by taking 48 hours to process. From there, Rachel would be able to make a healthier, more rational decision based on her needs and priorities.

The next day, Rachel skipped class in order to wait by the phone for her ex's promised phone call. As the clock hit 11pm without a phone call, Rachel was distraught over yet another rejection and cried herself to sleep over the lost relationship.

The next day, out of a pathetic sense of desperation, Rachel decided to cyber stalk her ex and sign on to his AOL buddy list and snoop around. Rachel, seeing a screen name that she didn't recognize started a conversation to do a little detective work. Through the conversation, Rachel realized that the girl that she was talking to was also the girl that was currently sleeping with her ex. After this tragic revelation, Rachel immediately signed off under the heavy burden of anxiety and stress.

The next day Rachel got a call from her ex, berating her about violating his privacy. He seemed to take great delight in telling her how sad and desperate she had seemingly become.

By signing on to the buddy list, Rachel left herself wide open to a knockout punch, followed by the humiliation of getting kicked while she was down. Rachel lost a lot of her dignity and personal leverage by allowing herself to become the bad guy in the situation with her blatant violation of her ex's privacy. In addition, she allowed her ex the satisfaction of realizing that Rachel was not only far from getting over the breakup, but that she was willing to sacrifice all of her dignity for a glimmer of insight into her broken relationship

As time progressed over the next several weeks, Rachel continued to see her ex out at social gatherings and other events, and although the two hadn't spoken since the buddy list incident, the pain persisted inside of Rachel every time she caught a glimmer of her ex.

Rachel was to the point that she was constantly looking for her ex in every situation that she was involved in and everywhere she went. She started to become very anxious, and, ultimately, she decided that she had to put an end to her self-inflicting behavior before it completely overtook her consciousness. Luckily for Rachel, she was going home from college for the summer and would have the luxury of enforced separation and disassociation.

Unfortunately for many of us during a breakup, you may not have the luxury of a compulsory separation. You will have to impose many of these restrictions upon yourselves, requiring a strong sense of internal discipline that Rachel obviously needed and wasn't able to obtain. In Rachel's case, it was crucial that she change her routine in order to avoid the anxiety stimulating situations involving her ex.

If Rachel were able to avoid these situations, she would have been able to maximize her opportunities at recovery from her break up. As logical as it seems to attempt to avoid situations with your ex, it can be very difficult, and Rachel didn't possess the strength at the time to perform this important step in recovery.

With the time and support that Rachel was able to receive at home during her summer vacation, compounded with a stringent diet of the Breakup Plan, Rachel was able to go back to school with a more functional state of mind in order to continue her resurgence toward the individual that she was prior to her relationship.

The time apart allowed Rachel to focus on the negative aspects of her relationship and accept the fact that the glamorization of her memories was only hindering her progress and prevention of entering into a similarly dysfunctional relationship.

Rachel deleted her technological ties to her ex, and identified her mother as her DL, in order to focus completely on the task at hand. When you are handed a gift such as Rachel's obligatory vacation, you must take advantage, and make the most of it. Heal, take time, and realize that sometimes you have to seize the moment and take advantage of a little bit of luck and good fortune. Luck, or even fate (depending on your view of the universe) may appear to each individual differently, but if and when it does, you must take advantage of the opportunity to use it in order to get over your ex. Rachel got lucky, seized the moment and followed the Breakup Plan. RACHEL DID IT AND SO CAN YOU!!!!

3

Change Your Routine

One of the nicest parts of a relationship is the routines and habits that you have come to enjoy with your ex. Whether or not you meant to form these habits, the phone calls or kiss before bed, the bars and restaurants you frequent, the meetings in the hall, courtyard etc., and even the friends and circles that you have run with through your relationship, are all part of the routine that you are no longer a part of.

One of the hardest things to get used to is the ending of the goodnight or good morning text or call with your ex, but it is often the simplest of routine activities that are the hardest to let go of, and the text is one of the hardest patterns to break. No matter how hard, it is very important that you begin to become invisible to your ex, and ceasing from daily texting or calling is a great way to get the point that you are no longer compelled to participate in this ritual across to your ex.

Often times, it is hard to navigate and identify what behaviors were yours before the relationship started, however, identification of your own routine is a very important aspect of your rediscovery of who you are. It is very important that you identify the routines that you shared with your ex in order to make sure that you are able to avoid these things, at least temporarily. Taking control of your routine is just another small way to gain independence over your daily routine and life.

One of the really unfair parts of a breakup is the loss of friends that you have become close with via your ex, and it sucks to have to give them up. The reality of this is the fact that, in most occasions, the allegiance of these gained friends will almost always lie with your ex, no matter how strong your bond may have become with them throughout your relationship.

It is also likely that there are friends of yours from the past that you have lost touch with during your relationship with your ex.
Unfortunately, this happens to most of us at some point, and while this is often a mistake, it is not one that can't or usually won't be forgiven. Your true friends will be there for you during the hard times, and often reaching out to them, will be enough to rekindle the friendship.

Since you are most likely going to have to sever the ties with the friends you made through your ex, there is no better opportunity to restart your relationships with the friends that you have lost touch with.

It always hurts to see your ex in a capacity of anything other than your boyfriend/girlfriend, and for this reason, not seeing them in any capacity, is the best way to get over them. Seeing your ex's friends can also be difficult at the beginning of a breakup because of all of the memories that each one of these people once held for you, not to mention the temptation to talk about the breakup with these friends is almost impossible to avoid.

There is nothing that worse than seeing your ex's friends, telling him or her about how much you miss them, and all of the time you are spending thinking about, and pining over your relationship. Remember, perception is the key, and it is crucial that your ex believe that you are doing well without them.

Information that states the opposite will only prolong the time it takes to get over the breakup, and give your ex a sense of satisfaction that they are still in control of the relationship and your emotions that they have not earned or deserve.

There are important steps that you can take immediately to avoid some of these difficulties. They start with walking to class differently, parking your car in a different spot, frequenting a different hangout and altering any situation that would involve a potential awkward run in with your ex. If you hear that your ex will be somewhere that you were planning on going to, change your plans. If there is a chance that your ex will show up at the party you are supposed to attend, change your plans.

"But why should I have to change my life and routine when the breakup is their fault?" you may be asking. Well, the answer to this is not the easiest pill to swallow, because in theory, you are right. It isn't fair that you have to do all of the work when the breakup wasn't your choice in the first place, but as we all know; "Life isn't Fair," and for this reason, you are the one who has to step up and do the work that is necessary to getting through this breakup.

While it will be hard and annoying at times to change your routine and plans when necessary, the payoff is well worth the cost. Not only will it help you, but it will make your ex not only question his or her decision, but show them just how strong your resolve is. Even if untrue, it will imply that you could care less about the break up.

Wouldn't that feel great? To be in control and to make your ex feel hurt and vulnerable for once. This is a great opportunity to make a statement for everyone around you to realize that you are strong, confident and over him/her. Walk a new path, and let your ex follow your footsteps once and for all.

4

Look Away

No matter where you go, there your ex is. On your desk, in your wallet, on your locker door, as your computer wallpaper, on your Facebook or MySpace page, you may be following them on twitter, yahoo messenger etc., they are constantly staring at you reminding you of the good times and the love the two of you once had together. But it's time to face the fact that those times are over, and it's time to take down the pictures. Here we go...

1. Get yourself a box and some good packing tape.

2. Take any picture, stuffed animal, piece of jewelry or any other reminder of your ex and place it in the box.
3. Grab that packing tape and seal that bad boy as tight as possible.
4. Place that box in a closet, garage, basement, attic, or anywhere that it won't stare you down on a daily basis tempting you to indulge in the memories of the past.

As a professional and someone who has been through just what you're going through, I can testify that it's important to not throw away or even burn the box because it is essential to keep the physical memories of your relationship for later use.

Eventually, these items will be a sense of entertainment and reminders of what you want and don't want in your future relationships. They will, also, be a lifelong reminder of how strong you are as a person to have gotten through such a hard time and moved on to bigger and better things.

The idea of looking away is not only a literal one, but a figurative idea as well. When you see a person, picture, tree, statue, or any such object you keep a mental picture in your mind of that image. But once you look away, that mental picture immediately starts to fade. Slowly you start to forget details about the image, and then one day you can no longer remember anything about it.

The same holds true for a picture of your ex. Maybe you've had the experience with someone in the past. As you take time away from them, you start to forget what they look and even sound like. The fading of your ex's image is a metaphor for the fading of the passionate feelings that will ultimately dwindle as you move on to new relationships with friends as well as new boyfriends or girlfriends.

Look away, because taking your eyes off of your ex, literally and figuratively, will allow you to open yourself up to becoming aware of the vast amounts of other fish in the sea. Forgive me for the cliché, but it really is true.

It is almost impossible to fathom being with someone else right now, but take it from a victim of the same emotional crime that has been committed against you; you are the new hot commodity. Although you may never have realized it, there are people that have been checking you out, waiting and hoping for you to be single again.

Think about this for a second: all the time that you have been in an unhealthy relationship, there have been others hoping for the time that they could ask you out *(just take my word for it, I'm a professional)*. You have to take advantage of the freedom and power of being single, and remember that there are so many people to meet, get to know, and possibly date right in your school, youth group, job, Greek system etc.

Looking away from your ex opens you up to the opportunity of a lifetime. This will give you the opportunity to grow spiritually and socially, and reclaim the person that you were before your lost relationship. On the next page you will see an exercise called guided imagery. Guided imagery has been shown to be helpful with patients who have undergone major surgeries, or who have suffered a major loss or shock (such as a breakup).

The explanation of why this works is basically that positive imagery is visualized flowing through the body along with measured breathing, and together, visualizing relaxation while meditating can bring relief. Follow the instructions and the guided imagery on the next page to begin to feel a sense of relaxation and control. Think about the person you were before your relationship for a second. It's time to reclaim yourself and move forward. Look away, and start to notice new and better opportunities.

Guided Imagery for a Breakup[1]

The following is one of the guided imagery scripts you can use; it should simply be read slowly into a tape recorder, with long pauses at the end of each paragraph. You can then play the script back for a short visualization session whenever you have a few moments of free time and a quiet place to be alone.

It's time to relax, time to let all the worry of the day drift away. You are seated comfortably, and are about to consciously relax all of your muscles, one by one. Start with your hands. Let your fingers go limp... now your palms... now your wrists. Your forearms are completely relaxed now, and your elbows... your shoulders... and your back.

Relax the muscles in your face. Your eyelids droop shut... the tension goes out of your neck. Your hips are loose and your thighs... your knees... your calves. Now your feet are going limp, every toe is relaxing. You are completely

---

[1] Information obtained from www.selfesteem2go.com

relaxed from head to toe. Breathe slowly and deeply from your diaphragm ten times, counting five on each inhale, and five on each exhale.

In your mind, open your eyes. Ahead of you, there is a door, centered in the wall about ten steps away from you. You are going to walk towards that door, and with each step the worries and anxieties you are dealing with in your life will drift further and further away until all you see is the door.

Are you ready?

Take one slow step towards the door. One: Take another step. Two: Another. Three: As you near the door, it begins to glow softly. Four: It is a warm, welcoming light, like soft sunshine. Five: The door is beginning to swing open. Six: Through the door is light. Seven: Through the door is warmth. Eight: Through the door is safety. Nine: You are about to step through the door. Ten: You are standing, looking through the door at a beautiful beach. Step through the door, and shut it behind you. The sun is warm… the sand is soft… you can hear waves breaking on the shore. Walk slowly down the beach, enjoying the gentle breeze and thinking about how lovely it is to be so relaxed and carefree…

(Leave some space on the tape blank, or fill in with a recording of nature sounds such as waves and seagulls. This can last as long as you wish a session to be.)

It's been a lovely walk on the beach, and now you see a door about ten steps away, coming into shape.

Are you ready?

Ten: When you walk through the door, you will be energized.
Nine: When you walk through the door, you will be well rested.
Eight: When you walk through the door, you will feel ready for the day.
Seven: On the other side of that door is the world you left.
Six: However, it has subtly changed in your absence.
Five: It is a softer, calmer version of the world.
Four: There is nothing in that world you cannot handle.
Three: You will have a wonderful day.
Two: Are you ready? One… step through the door and open your eyes.

Welcome back!

Can't Get Enough

We all have known couples that have broken up at least ten times and keep getting back together, regardless of how miserable they make each other. It's not that the addiction to their ex is more powerful than others who are able to break it off more expediently; it's usually the fact that the serial re-connector is involved with a boyfriend or girlfriend that is a master manipulator. This happens whether they are aware of the emotional exploitation or not.

It is also very difficult for people in these types of situations to identify the destructive nature of the on and off nature of their relationship. The emotional roller coaster employed during this lack of stability is one of the most damaging emotional conundrums a person can go through.

Unfortunately, usually the person being hurt the most is always the one who has blind faith in the pot of gold at the end of the rainbow. The hope that this will finally be the time that things work out and they can finally be the couple that appears in his or her fantasies. This emotional burden is the backbone of the struggle that the next three cases employ. A fear of being alone, coupled with a laundry list of emotional baggage, and a sense of comfort within the relationship, can be a very destructive combination.

Sam and Julie's relationship began as so many relationships do. The two met at a party, hooked up, and began to date shortly there after. There wasn't any official discussion about their relationship, but it just became common knowledge that the two were together, exclusively. For a year things progressed well, blossoming into a very loving, healthy relationship. Sam was a musician and Julie a sorority girl. Although the two got along very well, they had very little in common other than the fact that they ran in similar social groups and had a good time together.

After a year in the relationship, Sam committed himself more intensely to his music, without the full support of Julie. Although Julie was very excited to see Sam on stage and indulged in being the performer's girlfriend, she was often somewhat threatened by Sam's new-found celebrity and talent. Julie's insecurity was cancelled out by a discovered sense of confidence from Sam, who began to find that he had an appetite for the attention of other girls. Sam, however, being the gentleman that he was continued to remain faithful, although his hunger for new love continued to strengthen.

Sam had decided to study abroad in Australia, and felt as though the time was right to end his relationship with Julie. Sam craved the independence and was concerned with the idea of monogamy as he contemplated his ability to remain faithful while so far away. The two separated for the six month period, but, ultimately, remained faithful to the idea of reconciliation once Sam got back into town.

The problem with the beginning of this breakup is the fact that the severance of their relationship was without any form of commitment on either end. It's like attempting to stop smoking but still buying a carton of cigarettes. The temptation to return to the habit is too strong to be able to effectively quit, and the same holds true for the sort of half break that Sam and Julie engaged in. It would have been best to have formulated an effective plan of action, whether that is to stay faithful or break up, the couple should have made a decision that did not allow them to hang in limbo for the six months.

While in Australia, Sam dated several girls and enjoyed his freedom while continuing to keep in close contact with Julie via e-mail and phone, ultimately, contributing to a heightened sense of anxiety and stress over his behavior for both of them, while abroad. While Sam was in Australia, Julie attended a summer camp as a staff member and engaged in her own relationship with a new guy. When the six - month separation period was over, both Sam and Julie reunited after their relational hiatus, feeling a sense of nervousness and uncertainty regarding their relationship.

Due to the ambiguity of the separation between Sam and Julie, neither person was able to fully commit to any other potential partner, as well as setting up an anxiety induced situation when returning from their separation by setting up a situation where neither person could be totally honest about each respective trip without hurting the other's feelings.

There was a noticeable sense of awkwardness when the two reunited, because both members of the couple were uncertain about their relational future. The two went back and forth as if nothing had changed, but, ultimately, things had changed. Julie, feeling a strong disconnect from Sam, ultimately, ended the relationship stating that she needed to be on her own for a while and consequently dealing Sam a considerable ego blow.

This move by Julie would have been a smart, effective decision if she would have been able to stick to her plan, and move on to new possible dating partners.

Sam continued to feel upset and hurt, and pined for any opportunity he could have to speak, see, or run into Julie. After several weeks, and Sam effectively beginning to regain control over his emotions and life, Julie decided that she would like to give the relationship another chance. Like clockwork, the two fell right back into the relationship, now saddled with a considerable amount of baggage and ammunition for future fights and problems.

As discussed in earlier chapters, it is usually around the time of a person beginning to recover from their breakup that reconciliation is sought from the other member of the dissolved relationship. The hurt that the person that had been broken up is saddled with, often, allows for an easy relational reconciliation, without any contemplation of whether reconciliation is in the best interest for the couple.

Throughout the next year, the relationship progressed with an obvious disconnect between the couple. Julie wanted to be serious and exclusive, and Sam, ultimately, dated with the idea that the couple would end their relationship after graduation at the end of the year. The couple shared a lot of the same friends, and ran with very similar circles, allowing for a codependent relationship to evolve in which competition and demanding behavior had become the norm.

When Sam would go out, Julie would have to go out with her friends. If Sam went out of town, Julie would go out of town with her friends. Each time, setting up a tit for tat situation where it was unlikely that there would be a winner, and more likely that neither Sam, nor Julie, would end up feeling happy about the situation. In addition to the face to face contact, the couple had a lot of contact through instant messaging and texting, only adding to the constant sense of contact and codependence.

After graduation, Sam planned to move to California, with Julie hoping to receive an invite to join him. Sam followed through with his plan to split up after graduation and unfortunately for Julie, the invitation to join Sam in California never came, but the couple continued to be in close contact through the use of both their cell phones and internet. Both Sam and Julie understood that the other person had the freedom and opportunity to date others, yet both Sam and Julie resented the idea of this happening. There was a lot of jealousy, manipulation and anxiety on both ends, relative to the thought that the other was dating someone new.

Again, the continued contact after the breakup only invited negative feelings and anxiety on both ends. Neither Sam nor Julie were feeling or gaining any sense of satisfaction, but the unhappiness that the couple felt was so ingrained in their routine, that the fear of separation became larger than a normal breakup. The couple was so embedded in each others life that they could no longer view their future without each other, no matter how miserable they each were.

The pattern of misery continued for another year with an on again and off again routine that never allowed either Sam or Julie to begin to get over one another. Whenever the two would finally decide to end the relationship, within several weeks either Sam or Julie would call; text, e-mail, etc., and the unhealthy pattern would again start up. Each time the relational wound deepened and the anxiety was exacerbated.

Ultimately, Julie decided that enough was enough and decided to officially put an end to the on again and off again pattern the two had engaged in for so long. Sam was devastated, feeling a sense of loss and insecurity, and not understanding how to begin to heal from the breakup because it was so out of his routine and knowledge base. Sam had no idea how to move on when the couple had been faced with the same situation so many times with a very different outcome. Up until now, the couple had always reconciled, Sam had never been forced to actually get over a relationship.

If this were the end of the story, this would have been a great relational gift to give to Sam. Julie could have finally bailed out both Sam AND herself from the dysfunctional pattern that had consumed each other's lives for so long, allowing each to finally move on and recover.

Each time that Sam began to recover from the break up, Julie would send an ambiguous e-mail or text asking how Sam was, or informing him about something important in her life, each time reopening the relational wound in Sam's heart.

The messages that Julie kept leaving for Sam kept him constantly confused about her motives and reasons for the contact, especially because the messages never involved any form of relational discussion or conversation. Had Sam deleted the messages before reading them, while being forced to identify that Julie had sent him a message, the identification would have been immeasurably easier to overcome, than the confusion that afflicted Sam after each ambiguous message.

The cycle of randomized e-mails continued until Sam finally decided to put an end to the manipulation and destructive on again and off again behavior. Sam decided to finally delete Julie's number from his phone, her screen name from his buddy list, and removed her from his MySpace and Facebook friends.

The recovery process was difficult for Sam, and he did continue to receive the occasional text or e-mail from Julie, but he never responded and was able to handle and view these attempts at contact as just a continued manipulation…a way for Julie to ensure that she wouldn't be forgotten. Sam's adoption of the Breakup Plan allowed him to finally move on from the hurt of his breakup, and although it still bothers him to reflect on his relationship, he has been able to completely remove Julie from his everyday thoughts and has lived to successfully date again.

His friends have actually given him the nickname Magneto due to the ease with which he meets girls. The Breakup Plan allowed Sam to be where he is now, if only he would have started to follow it sooner. SAM DID IT AND SO CAN YOU!!!!

5

Your DL

One of the most important aspects of recovery is the ability to talk, vent, cry, yell and let out all of your emotions toward your break up to anyone that will listen. The problem with this is that, although people may care for you very deeply, they probably are already sick and tired of hearing about your ex and or your break up.

In addition to wearing down your friends, you also increase the chance of your ex getting word of all of your emotions and feelings, which as far as I'm concerned, is a terrible thing. Why let them into your emotional world and thoughts? That ship has sailed and they let it go, along with the ability to know what you are thinking.

For all of these reasons, you have a very important decision to make, like whom are you going to choose to be your *Designated Listener (DL)*. Your DL is the one and only person that you are going to discuss your breakup, and or any other feelings associated with your ex. It is important to choose a person very close to you, whether it is a family member or friend, but it has to be someone with virtually no association with your ex or his or her friends.

When picking your DL, it is crucial to explain to the person that you have selected them to be your DL and would like to know if they would accept the position. It is important to let your DL realize how important his or her job will be, and that it is a vital part of getting over your ex.

This person is going to be your rock to bang ideas, feelings and possibly your head against. Your DL has to be someone that doesn't mind hearing the same stories over and over again (because we both know that's what they're going to hear) and it has to be someone who will help you to work through the steps outlined in this book.

Your DL is there to be a tool in your shed of coping abilities, to maximize your ability to disassociate from your ex, and ultimately get over your break up. Pick carefully and deliberately in order to feel confident and empowered by your DL. Allow this person to be the personal touch that this book cannot supply you with, and to provide you with a real outlet for your emotional baggage.

Since every breakup is slightly different, the particular conversations that you will have with your DL will vary, but it is important that your DL is a person that can challenge you and get you out of your head. What I mean by this is you want to find a person that can take your irrational, anxious thoughts, and put them in a logical, rational perspective.

Because of this, you may want to pick someone who is not overly dramatic or emotional. You have plenty of these qualities at the moment for the two of you, and you don't want your recovery to be interrupted by unneeded, unnecessary drama.

While it might sound lame, when choosing my own DL, the only person that seemingly fit all of the requirements was my mom. While she was probably more emotionally invested in me getting better than most, she was a constant ally in the fight that was being waged between my heart and my head.

I knew that she was a rational confidant; one that could help me make sense of my illogical thoughts (*like that my ex was just going through a phase, or that my anxiety was making me feel like I was having a heart attack*) and also a person who would never share the information and emotions that I was working through, with my ex.

My mom was there for me, morning, noon, or night, and I knew that I could count on her to listen to the same stories and concerns, over, and over, and over again. My mom was the perfect DL, and she personified all of the qualities that you should look for in your DL.

You may ask yourself the question, "What if my DL can't be reached and I really need to talk to someone?" There are several things that you can do to fill the void while you wait for your DL. The first is the obvious answer, yet not always the best, which is to call another one of your close friends or family members and talk to them. You can identify a person as a backup DL, and inform them ahead of time that you may be calling, texting, e-mailing, etc. them at some point, but it will only be in an emergency. This can often be enough to get you over the proverbial hump.

A second option, and one of my favorites, is to go online and find a breakup message board or website. http://messageboards.ivillage.com/iv-rlbreaking is a favorite of mine, and will give you plenty of opportunity to commiserate with other people going through the same emotions and hardship as you.

Finding your DL is a crucial step to recovery and one that I know you can do. Remember, confidence is the key, and limiting your emotional exchanges to your DL, will give you the opportunity to vent, while still appearing as though you are doing well to everyone else. Now go choose your DL, and let the venting begin.

It Just Feels Comfortable

Often times, in a relationship comfort become the most important aspect in keeping the couple together. Unfortunately, love, respect, modesty, and trust often times are allowed to take a back seat to familiarity and fear. Because of this, couples end up staying together way longer than necessary or even healthy. This next story is one of the most blatant examples of what I call the *familiarity phenomenon.*

Zoey met Izzy on the first day of orientation at a small college in the northeast. The two immediately hit it off, and basically began a relationship from the first day of classes. The two were immediately exclusive and happily together non-stop. Zoey and Izzy made friends together, with Izzy joining a fraternity and enjoying having Zoey on his arm at all of the functions and parties. Since the college was so small, it was very difficult for the two to make a lot of friends outside of their initial social circle, and their social lives essentially revolved around one another. Compounded with the size of the school was the fact that both Zoey and Izzy lived in the same dorm, adding to the availability and acceleration of their relationship.

After the first year however, things in the relationship began to change. Izzy began to present himself with a sense of arrogance and bravado, and compounded with Zoey's lack of confidence, these new behaviors began acting as a catalyst to fighting between the couple and a loss of trust. As the relationship gradually deteriorated, and the couple became more and more combative, Izzy and Zoey's friends began taking sides, fueling the relational fire.

Izzy started to stay out without calling Zoey. He was outwardly flirting with other girls. Because he was aware of Zoey's lack of confidence in herself, Izzy knew that no matter what happened in the relationship, he could always count on Zoey being there when and however he wanted her.

As you are reading this, you should be picking up on the instability of the emotional relationship, which, ultimately, acted as glue that kept the physical relationship ever present. Because Zoey had become so reliant on and comfortable in the relationship, her sense of confidence and individuality had deteriorated, making it extremely easy for Izzy to do whatever he pleased in the relationship. Although I can't categorize a lack of confidence as a mistake, it is, however, something that needs to be very closely looked at while reading this story.

Eventually, the relationship became too much for either of them to handle, and Izzy initiated a breakup. Although neither person felt satisfied with the closure, or lack there of that they received, they agreed to put an end to the relationship for good. The irony in this statement is the fact that as you will soon read, the complete opposite of a breakup is what ensued.

Zoey and Izzy decided to not call each other and allow time to heal each person's emotional wounds, but as the summer quickly approached, Izzy took the first step to ensuring that the relationship would fall into an on again and off again pattern. Izzy called Zoey, after only a week of being broken up, and invited her to come to his beach house for a weekend trip with his family. Although reluctant, Zoey agreed, hoping that spending time together in a familial situation would help to bring the couple closer and, ultimately, back together.

This was a huge mistake. Although very understandable, being only a week removed from the breakup, it allowed Izzy to continue to flex his emotional control over the relationship, and only contribute to the possibility of further pain and humiliation for Zoey. Zoey should have declined nicely and wished Izzy a good trip, no matter how hard and depressing the weekend alone might have been.

During the weekend, Izzy was disrespectful and carried himself with an angry subtlety that Zoey didn't understand. Why had Izzy invited Zoey for the weekend if he planned on acting as awkwardly and inappropriately as he was? The answer was unknown to Zoey, but at the end of the weekend, the couple had not only gained a fresh sense of resentment for each other, but there was a contemptuous vibe that was floating around the idea of their entire relationship.

As expected by both, the couple continued to be in contact over the phone and e-mail throughout the summer and both returned to school in a state of relational limbo. Not together, not broken up, but definitely on two different wavelengths. Izzy's wavelength included the mind frame that the two would continue a physical relationship at his convenience. Meanwhile, Zoey was under the impression that the bond between the two was strong enough to get over the past hurt and betrayal. "It was a new year and new chance for us."

Good couples don't break up!!!! The fact that Zoey and Izzy continued to interact as a couple (be that as it may, a dysfunctional one) allowed each person to ignore the past problems and glamorize their current situation as one that could be functional and happy. The fact that neither person allowed for closure and was persistent with it, permitted the couple to keep relying on the familiarity of each other, especially in Zoey's case.

Each time the couple spent time together; Zoey was permitted to believe in a fantasy that her and Izzy were on the mend and would ultimately be back together. Zoey allowed herself to be victimized over and over again by permitting Izzy to have her whenever he saw fit.

The relationship continued this way for several months. Izzy would call Zoey when he wanted company, and ignore her when he didn't. This went on until the time that Izzy started a new relationship with another girl. Unfortunately for Zoey, Izzy didn't inform her of his new relationship until Zoey was forced to view the relationship in action at a bar several weeks later when she saw Izzy with his new girlfriend.

Obviously distraught over the situation, Zoey became irate and belligerent. She even caused a massive outburst and scene in the bar. Ultimately, Zoey stormed out and ran home; leaving Izzy with the satisfaction that he still controlled the emotional side of Zoey.

This personifies the importance of appearing together and confident in all social situations revolving around your ex. Although understandable and justified in her reaction, Zoey not only looked pathetic in front of all of her friends, but she allowed Izzy to once again control her emotional state and then revel in his conquest over Zoey's heart. Can you imagine the shock on Izzy's face if Zoey would have remained calm and just decided to leave without a scene? I can almost assure you that Izzy would have been devastated over the lack of response from Zoey.

After several weeks of recuperation from the humiliation of the scene at the bar, Zoey met a new guy with whom she started to date casually. They enjoyed each other's company and had a lot in common. Unfortunately, just as things began to relationally heat up, Izzy caught word that Zoey had found a new person to date. Predictably, since his new relationship had fizzled, he confronted Zoey about her new relationship. Zoey, although tempted by Izzy's advances, rejected Izzy and continued on with her relationship.

That night, while out at the bar, Zoey and Izzy ran into each other, and this time Zoey wasn't as confident in her ability to ignore Izzy's flirting. Zoey, ultimately, gave in, ending up back with Izzy at his apartment. Once again, they were repeating the cycle, that up until that night, Zoey had been working hard to break.

Izzy, sensing a loss of control over Zoey, now that she had found a new person to date, manipulated a fragile Zoey in order to regain control. Allowing Izzy back into her life, Zoey totally reversed any progress that she had made over the past several weeks. The fact that it was so easy for Izzy to get back into Zoey's life not only empowered Izzy, but totally diminished any pride and respect for herself that Zoey may have regained. Ex's, often times, have a very difficult time when you decide to move on with your life, and they will do just about anything to regain control and power.

The need for the comfort of the relationship outweighed the rational fact that rekindling the relationship would be destructive and have a negative effect on Zoey's gentle frame of mind.

This destructive pattern repeated itself for several more years, continuing to the point that Izzy and Zoey had burned themselves out on one another. Zoey had been so beaten down and abused by the rollercoaster ride of her relationship that she no longer had the ability to understand what a healthy relationship could look like, and this, ultimately, skewed her view on men.

In due course, the couple once again ran into each other at a bar after several months of being apart. Again the two hooked up, but this time rather than a resurgence of emotional attachment and comfort, the reconnection of the two brought Zoey a sense of depression and self doubt about her ability to ever fully recover from her relationship with Izzy.

The main issue, other then the fact that Zoey kept struggling to stay away from Izzy, was the emotional strain that each new encounter was placing on her, and ultimately the power that she continued to give to Izzy.

Unfortunately for Zoey, she wasn't strong enough to reject Izzy's advances, and although no longer in love with Izzy, there was still a sense of control over her life that she no longer had power of. The added sense of depression could have been completely avoided had Zoey personified the confidence and strength to realize that she was a strong woman who deserved better than what Izzy was giving her.

Luckily for Zoey, this was the last time that she would see Izzy. Following this last encounter, Zoey picked up the Breakup Plan and began to work the program. She cut all ties with Izzy, removed him from her phone, buddy list, and Facebook friends, and worked extremely hard to avoid any situation in which she may run into Izzy. After several months of self reflection, physical healing, and working the steps, Zoey was finally able to tell the story of her relationship with a smile on her face.

After Zoey finished telling me her complete story, she told me that discussing it from start to finish was a cathartic experience. She felt cleansed, unburdened, and finally realized how pathetic she was during her on again and off again relationship with Izzy. Although, Zoey ultimately was able to get over her ex, had she began to follow the Breakup Plan sooner, who knows what opportunities may have been presented to her?

Whether that could have been a new boyfriend, traveling opportunity, or just a great memory, because of her complete involvement in her relationship she was unable to have any of these experiences.

Today, Zoey is doing great and credits much of her success to the Breakup Plan and the empowering words and steps that it contains. We all learn things from our breakups. It just took Zoey longer than necessary. It is time to take the steps to get over your ex. Do not lose time and opportunities like Zoey. ZOEY DID IT AND SO CAN YOU!!!!

6

Occupy Your Time

A difficult aspect of getting over a breakup, that is often overlooked, is the importance of occupying your time with positive, constructive activities. Because your thoughts often times have a way of lets say, "Gaining a life of their own," it's crucial to find ways to stop your brain from wandering off into the "la-la land" of pining and dwelling on your ex and what went wrong.

I'm sure you have done this about a thousand times by now, and I bet you still haven't come up with an answer. Unfortunately, trying to figure out the reason, or moment, or situation, that led to the breakup, is something that you will be unable to accomplish, and, therefore, will only perpetuate the difficulty in getting over this. What you need to do is set aside several minutes a day to allow yourself to not only grieve your relationship, but to reflect on where you would like to be mentally at the end of the day.

It's important to allow yourself this time because the more you try to suppress the feelings about your relationship, the more they will pop into your head. It is as close to a guarantee as I will give you, but the more you try to stop doing something, the more intensely you want to do that exact thing. Think about the parent who tells their child that they can't play outside... Now, all the kid wants to do is go outside, even if they didn't want to in the first place.

The same holds true for adults, especially during a breakup, the difference being, however, that it is double trouble. What I mean by this is that the first difficulty in this scenario is that we always want what we can't have, and secondly, the more we tell ourselves that we can't have something, the more we want it. You see the dilemma?

There is absolutely nothing wrong with thinking, grieving, or even temporarily dwelling on your relationship. However, your actions have to contradict your feelings. While you may be grieving, dwelling, pining, etc., you have to begin to occupy your time with activities that have nothing to do with your breakup. Your thoughts may be in breakup land, but your actions have to be in that of the real world.

The rest of your idle time during the day needs to be spent by participating in activities that will occupy your mind. Whether it be playing sports, an instrument, going to the mall, working, journaling, meditating, working out, or any other positive behavior, you must fill your day with something other than sitting and thinking.

Allow yourself to escape the trap of your obsessive brain and get something done. Get out of bed, take a shower, turn of the depressing music, put on something nice to wear that makes you feel good, and get out of the house. If you're religious, discovering a greater sense of spirituality is often helpful in tough times such as a breakup and any form of positive growth will only strengthen your desire to overcome your ex and relationship. This may mean going to Church or Synagogue, picking up a book on Zen philosophies, or any number of other spiritual options.

In addition to taking your mind off of your relationship, the time spent on positive activities will make you a stronger, more well-rounded and ultimately, a more positive person. From the loss of your relationship must come personal growth and understanding.

How upset is your ex going to be when he or she realizes that not only are you not dwelling on them, but you are actually becoming a better person? As important as it is to take all of these steps for your own personal growth, everyone knows that it is also very satisfying to see your ex long for you now that you're not available. There is no better revenge in the world than being unavailable to your ex, especially now that you are allowing yourself to be off the market for just one specific person. The perpetrator of this emotional crime: Your Ex.

The next thing that I would like you to do is to buy a date book, or calendar that you can take with you everywhere that you go. This is going to be your designated, getting over a breakup calendar, and this is where you are going to record your scheduled activities that you will be participating in to ensure that your time is

It's Not Me, It's You!

occupied with things other than thinking about your breakup and your ex. The rationale behind this is simple; by taking an active role in planning and participating in activities to get over your breakup, this will allow you to take control over the situation, and become empowered, as opposed to victimized.

Giving yourself permission to begin moving away from your ex, both literally and figuratively, is a monstrous step in beginning to move on from this breakup. The more things that you can begin to schedule, and in turn record in your calendar, the less time you will have to think about your ex.

Each night before you go to bed, I want you to look at the calendar to see what the next day has in store for you, and all of the important and fun things that you have planned. The more things you have scheduled, the less time you will have to think about your ex. Plan your day, fill up your calendar, and begin to get over your ex. It's that simple!

7

Business Dealings

Often times during a relationship, you end up sharing expenses with your ex such as being on a family cell phone plan together, paying rent, car insurance and other such business partnerships. Why would I call it a business partnership when "What we shared was filled with feelings and emotions"… "We wanted to live together so we had to split the rent"… "We could have unlimited minutes to talk to each other if we shared a cell phone."

No matter what the emotions were that propelled you to share financial obligations, the fact of the matter is that now these shared expenses are one more obstacle to hurdle in order to get over this break up.

I talked earlier about the need to cool down your emotions the way that your ex has, by starting to view your relationship as a past experience; an experience to be learned from. Along this same theory is the view that all of your shared expenses are part of a business partnership that has dissolved and needs to be handled as if you were laid off from your job, but was still owed a paycheck.

Viewing these items as a business partnership allows you to attempt to depersonalize the sharing of objects and bills, and allows you to take the position of someone who is owed money, or needs to pay back the interest on a loan to the bank.

The most important thing about approaching the business aspect of your past relationship is to wait until you have had plenty of time to recover from the breakup. The reason for this is that the steps to tackling your business dealings with your ex are complicated and involve communication between the two of you, which is in direct opposition to everything that this book has told you thus far.

To handle this dissolved business partnership, it is important to do as much of the communicating between you and your ex through business type e-mails. It's extremely important to approach these e-mails with an amazing level of consciousness in order to keep your broken heart from expressing itself on screen.

Because I have stressed the importance of disassociating yourself completely, the only time that it is appropriate to have contact with your ex is to handle your mutual business. *Don't try to get away with it! I know what you're thinking!* "I can get in contact with my ex because we have to talk about our bills, and this will give me an opportunity to possibly reignite our relationship again or at lease discuss what went wrong." Bad thought... Bad Thought... BAD THOUGHT...

Although totally rational, you have to refrain from action. You can e-mail, but only if you can keep your e-mails short, sweet and to the point. Forget about any discussion of relational issues, because, ultimately, they will only force you to dwell on the past, and exacerbate your anxiety and depression.

If by chance you are forced to meet, or speak on the phone to handle your business, you must put on your poker face. If you learn nothing else from this chapter, you must take this to heart. You may be turning inside with anxiety, but you have to fake it. And let's remember, so much of these early steps require you to fake it, and fake it often. No matter how much you hurt or want to talk, deal with your business, deal with your business, deal with your business, and LEAVE!!!

Leave your ex wondering how you could possibly be doing so well after all you have been through. Leave them and let them watch you walk out of the room, with a smile on your face and your head held high. You've just been promoted from depressed, pathetic person, to confident, sexy ex girlfriend/boyfriend. Doesn't it feel great???

Pack Light

We all know couples that have been together on and off for a long time, continuously fighting about the same issues constantly. Each time the couple fights, they bring up past baggage, reliving every bad experience with every altercation. Relationships cannot be successful if past transgressions are rehashed on a daily basis, making it impossible to heal from past wounds. Although nobody expects to completely forget a past indiscretion, it is important to forgive and be able to move on to create new memories and experiences with your partner.

Without the ability to accomplish this feat, a couple will have a very difficult time reconnecting and having a successful relationship. This next story has all of the elements of a relationship full of baggage and bad memories, but unfortunately for the couple, they were unable to forgive and move on with their relationship in a positive direction.

Keith and Kelly met in high school when Kelly was a senior and Keith a junior. The two got along right from the start, and as in many high school relationships, were essentially exclusive from the start. The relationship continued successfully for the next two years with nothing more than the ordinary conflict and difficulties, until Kelly was ready to leave town to go to college and felt conflicted about her fidelity to Keith.

Due to her doubts in the relationship, Kelly decided to end the relationship, breaking Keith's heart. Keith, feeling upset and angry about the breakup took a vacation for several days with some friends, leaving the memories of Kelly at home for the time being.

Keith did exactly the right thing by disassociating from Kelly while he was digesting the idea of his breakup and trying to begin is life without his relationship.

Keith's vacation caused Kelly to have second thoughts about ending her relationship with Keith, and when Keith returned from vacation, Kelly was there waiting for him with open arms. The couple reunited and continued there relationship with a high level of satisfaction through their sophomore year of college. The two sharing many of each other's friends, as well as continuing to have an established group of friends from high school.

The summer of Kelly and Keith's sophomore year, Keith met a new girl from his work, and began a physical relationship with her. This launched a cycle of infidelity that both parties would be actively participating in.

When Kelly found out about Keith's unfaithfulness she ended the relationship. This left neither person satisfied, but allowed Keith to pursue other potential partners. Neither Keith nor Kelly, had ever had the opportunity to date other people in their lives, and although difficult, this was a great time for self exploration and a chance to see who else was out there.

Keith seized the moment, and with a carpe diem ("seize the day" in Latin) attitude, dated several girls, allowing him to figure out what he was looking for in a future partner. Unfortunately, the same was not true for Kelly, who was constantly consumed with the idea and fantasy that the two would, reconcile. Because of these thoughts, Kelly made herself available sexually whenever Keith wanted, and continued to stay moderately committed to a man that was no longer invested in the relationship.

What's unique about this story is the fact that Keith and Kelly at some point should have disassociated from the other permanently, but because of their lack of commitment to the breakup, they continued to hurt one another, creating a cyclical pattern of breaking up, with both parties initiating the temporary separation.

Most breakups are one sided, this one, however, cannot be categorized in the same manner because of the length of the relationship as well as the systematic sense of retaliation that contributed to the heavy baggage that continued to weigh the couple down.

The couple continued to remain in relational limbo, not together, but not fully broken up. This allowed for the instability of their relationship to ultimately affect the insecurity of Keith and Kelly. Towards the middle of their senior year, Keith and Kelly decided to once again begin a committed, exclusive relationship, with the hopes that the cycle of hurt could finally be put to rest.

Their happiness was short lived, with Kelly cheating on Keith, ending their relationship right in time for a major milestone in both of their lives, graduation. Keith and Kelly's families would be in town together to celebrate. One of the more interesting dynamics within the relationship was the fact that neither Keith nor Kelly kept their families informed about neither their relational problems nor the situation in general. So although the couple was involved in a very turbulent period of their relationship, they had to continue to appear happy and committed to each other.

The lack of honesty with their families was a symptom of their lack of honesty within themselves and with each other. Deep down, Keith and Kelly knew that their relationship was in a perpetual state of instability, but both people continued to lie to themselves, convincing each other that they could be happy, even with the amount of hurt and fear that the couple had instilled in each other. Had the couple allowed themselves to face the reality of their struggling relationship, they may have been able to put their misery behind them, and move on towards a happier more stable future, whether together or apart.

The evening of graduation, Kelly and Keith had a huge fight about all of their past indiscretions, including cheating, lying, and just an overall lack of respect and trust that the couple had grown to be accustomed to. As usual, the couple moved on from their fight the next day, with the residual hurt feelings remaining hidden just under the surface, available for resurfacing during their next fight. Shortly after graduation, Kelly moved out of town, and the couple decided to pursue a long distance relationship.

It's fascinating that Keith and Kelly were willing to attempt a long distance relationship, which for many couples can be more stressful than a traditional union. Their codependence on each other had grown so intense, that the couple was prepared to exacerbate the stress within their relationship in order to avoid terminating their emotional affiliation. Both Kelly and Keith were equally at fault for the continuation of their instability, both personally and relationally. Unfortunately, neither one had the guts to put an end to the pattern of misery nor perpetual hurt.

Over the next year the couple continued their relationship, only seeing each other several times, and, ultimately, getting along better than they had in a long time, contributing to a level of success that the couple hadn't experienced in years.

It's never a good indication for a relationship that has been continually strained to have their first level of success in years while only having contact several times over a period of a year. Although relational success should never be overlooked, it's important to focus on the context or situation with which the success lies, and a lack of contact is not necessarily an ideal situation to nurture a healthy relationship.

Based on their current success, Keith and Kelly decided to move in together when Keith started graduate school in the fall. The couple found an apartment, bought furniture, set up a family account on their cell phones, and for all intents and purposes followed the cohabitation (living together) script, hoping that happiness would follow. Unfortunately for the two, moving in together only intensified their animosity towards one another, as well as a damaging their communication and sexual relationship. The couple had become so unhappy that the only peaceful time in the relationship was when the two were apart.

Many couples believe that escalating their commitment, such as moving in together, or even marriage, will fix the issues within their relationship. Unfortunately, the opposite is usually what ensues, which is exactly what happened to Keith and Kelly. Had one of them decided to end their relationship, rather than continuing to deepen their illusion of commitment, both Keith and Kelly would not only have allowed more time for personal happiness, but could also have stopped the pattern of continual hurt that the couple continued to cycle through.

For a year and a half Keith and Kelly prolonged their unhappiness until Kelly decided to move back to her hometown. Although not identified as a way for the couple to start to separate, the inevitable was bound to happen. This separation, ultimately, resulted in the breakup of their relationship. This execution of the breakup came nearly six months after Kelly had moved away.

Keith, while visiting friends, got a late night phone call from Kelly who was breaking off the relationship with no specific reasoning other than the fact that the couple had been through too many conflicting situations to evolve into a successful, healthy couple. Although very hurt and blindsided by the breakup, Keith understood the breakup.

After eight years, Kelly had finally decided to end the vicious cycle that her and Keith had called a relationship. As difficult as it must have been to take the final step to initiate a relational termination, Kelly finally gave herself and Keith the greatest gift in the world: a chance to be happy and free from the burden of their continual conflict and hurt.

Because Kelly made the final decision to end the relationship, Keith was left dealing with the hurt and frustration of being forced to get over the breakup on someone else's terms. The blow to Keith's ego was substantial and it was extremely difficult for him to face the idea that he and Kelly were finished as a couple for good. Keith immediately contacted me for a Breakup Plan consultation. I placed Keith on the track to recovery, only several hours after his breakup.

It was unfortunate for Keith to have suffered through his relational conflict for so long, but through all of the discord, Keith finally understood the importance of reaching out for help while getting through a breakup. It would have been extremely beneficial for Keith to have consulted with me earlier in the relationship, but, ultimately, Keith made the right decision by beginning to follow the breakup steps immediately following his breakup.

Keith's situation was difficult because the couple shared financial resources as well as emotional bonds that had to be rearranged in order to start to move toward getting over the breakup. From the start, Keith took all of the prescribed steps: erasing Kelly's name from his phone, not e-mailing her, and allowing him the time to absorb the magnitude of his breakup. As expected, however, just as Keith was getting over Kelly, he received an e-mail from Kelly discussing her financial demands and requesting that Keith arrange for her to come to town and pick up her belongings.

Keith was lucky in the sense that he lived in a different city from Kelly, allowing him to be able to skip over some of the steps, specifically the step that involves changing his daily routine. However, even with the distance, the technology of today allowed for continuous manipulation by Kelly, which she disguised as a business deal.

With Keith in graduate school, Kelly was completely aware of Keith's financial issues, and took advantage of the fact that Keith needed money that was owed to him from past bills that the couple shared during their relationship.

The conflict from their relationship manifested itself through Kelly's continued manipulation of Keith's emotions by using finances to exert her control.

Utilizing his relational coaching, Keith eliminated much of the exploitation of his emotions by ensuring that any type of business transaction was dealt with over e-mail, and e-mail alone. Although the e-mails were difficult to read, the communication over the computer was much easier than subjecting him to hear Kelly's voice over the phone.

Ultimately, Keith continued to utilize the steps, completely disassociating himself from Kelly, and continuing to avoid any temptation to communicate with her. Shortly after the breakup, Keith met a new girl, and, ultimately, married her. Before this story ends however, Kelly provided Keith with one more bomb shell. Without any communication between the two in months, Kelly e-mailed Keith a message explaining that she was getting married and wished him the best for his life.

Kelly felt that it was necessary to exchange one more emotional blow in Keith's direction before completely committing herself to a new relationship. Knowing that this information would be received negatively by Keith, Kelly insisted on continuing to repeat the pattern of hurt, even after the relationship had ended.

Amazingly, Keith, although obviously upset, was able to see the positive aspect of the news of Kelly's engagement realizing that he had finally been granted permission to move on with his life without looking back.

So many times after a breakup, no matter how much time has passed, one, if not both of the members, still tease them with the idea that reconciliation may one day happen. Kelly allowed Keith to eliminate this fantasy as a possibility due to the permanence of Kelly's engagement. This was the first really generous act that Kelly had performed toward Keith in years, even if there were no altruistic motives involved. Sometimes the greatest gifts in the world are wrapped in very ugly packages.

Keith's reaction to the news of Kelly's engagement exemplified the progress that had been made in such a short time using the breakup plan. Keith is now in a serious, exclusive relationship and has not only moved into the acceptance stage, but has propelled himself to a level of satisfaction with his past relationship that only a person comfortable with himself and his life could achieve. Keith followed the Breakup Plan immediately following his breakup, and with guidance from a relationship coach, utilizing his DL, and following the advice from the steps, has been able to fully recover the aspect of his life that he had lost control of: his happiness. KEITH DID IT AND SO CAN YOU!!!

Conclusion

There are very few things in your young life that are as difficult as a traumatic breakup. Not having control over the status of your relationships, emotions, and even physical symptoms is a daunting and depressing situation that can be very hard to recover from.

There are so few resources for young adults that deal with the subject of breakups, and because of this, so much of your surrounding community has no way of understanding what you're going through. Your parents can't understand why you can't "just get over it," and your friends are busy taking sides, deciding who they are going to support. All of this leaving you isolated, in many ways, to handle the emotional burden of the breakup alone.

It is the isolation and lack of control that are the most important aspects to address in order to become empowered and confident. Getting control over your level of confidence and hurt are necessary in order to move toward a level of acceptance and positivism in relation to your ex.

The steps outlined in this book are common sense, practical solutions to allow you to expedite your recovery process from the trauma of your breakup. There are no profound ideas, just a proven, systematic guideline to empowerment and reclamation of your self confidence and control. After a breakup, it can often be impossible to know where to start on your journey to recovery. Hopefully, this book has provided you with a proven blueprint to resurgence and revitalization.

There was a lot of information outlined in this book, not all of which will apply to your situation; it is, however, important to utilize this book as a metaphorical support group by reading and studying the stories described in earlier chapters. You are not alone in what you are going through, and as long as you have this book, you will continue to have the support you need to get through this process.

I want to leave you with a true sense of confidence that I have in your ability to get over your breakup because of the confidence I have in the Breakup Plan. I am confident that the steps will work for you, and as long as you stay true to the relational script that I outlined, you will be successful.

The word success is really what is beautiful about relationships as a whole. Each couple, relationship, and situation is unique to each person, therefore allowing for a personal sense of what will be successful for each individual. The Breakup Plan allows for success to be achieved, no matter what that will, ultimately, mean for you. There will be tough times ahead, hiccups in your recovery, stumbling blocks in your way, but you CAN and WILL do this.

Define what success is for you, and use the steps to achieve that definition. Use this book as a crutch, and don't be ashamed to rely on it to help you through the tough situations that you are bound to encounter. Change your routine, use caution online, take your ex out of your phone, and change your life for the better. You can do this, I can help. You will feel better. You deserve it.

Allow yourself to be happy and let this book help. Now is the time to reclaim yourself, your personal identity, and your confidence. You deserve to be happy, and to, ultimately, feel satisfied in the relational decisions you will make in life. Now is the time: Carpe Diem. Seize the day, TODAY, to begin to recover and reclaim you. You can make it through this, this book can help. Now get back out there, start the program and begin your recovery. Others have done it, so can you!!!!

About the Author

Dr. Matt Borer is a Marriage and Family Therapist living in Jacksonville Florida with his wife Samantha and their two cats. Matt has a private practice specializing in couples and families and is a Professor of Psychology and Family Systems Theory. This book was inspired by Matt's difficult break-up as well as the strange and confusing breakups of the loved ones around him. He has articles published in English, Greek, and French, and has recently started *The Dr. Matt Project*; an initiative to start answering young adults questions about relationships and life in general. To find out more about Matt, please visit *www.mattborer.com*